Pet Dog

Written by Jean Coppendale

Collins

A pet dog is fun.

We can train a pet dog.

We train a pet dog to sit.

A pet dog sits. Pat the dog.

A pet dog runs and jumps.

We train a pet dog not to tug.

If we toss a stick a pet dog gets it.

We train a pet dog to run back.

A pet dog is fed on a mat.

A pet dog has a soft bed.

A pet dog licks a hand if we pat him.

A dog is the best pet.

Train a pet dog

Ideas for reading

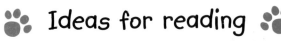

Written by Clare Dowdall BA(Ed), MA(Ed)
Lecturer and Primary Literacy Consultant

Learning objectives: read simple words by sounding out and blending the phonemes all through the word from left to right; read a range of familiar and common words and simple sentences independently; use phonic knowledge to write simple regular words; show an understanding of how information can be found in non-fiction texts to answer questions about where, who, why and how; use talk to organise, sequence and clarify thinking, ideas, feelings and events

Curriculum links: Understanding the World: The world

Focus phonemes: d, g, ck, b, f, ss, j, ai

Fast words: we, the

Word count: 88

Getting started

- Look at the front cover together and discuss what the story might be about.

- Read the title on the front cover and ask children to talk about their pets and experiences with pet dogs.

- Read the blurb together. Help children to sound out each phoneme and blend them to read each word fluently. Talk about what the word *train* means. Ask children if they have helped to train a dog, and what we train dogs to do.

Reading and responding

- Open the book and turn to pp2–3. Model how to read the text, blending phonemes and noting the punctuation.

- Ask children to continue to read. Support them as they read aloud, helping them to decode longer words with adjacent consonants, e.g. train, jumps.

- Pause at p8. Look at this longer sentence together and model how to read it using the punctuation.

- Ask children to continue reading to the end of the book, noticing interesting facts about pet dogs.